COMMUNICATION MASTERY

COMMUNICATION MASTERY

42 TECHNIQUES FOR WORKPLACE SUCCESS

JASMINE WILLIAMS

TABLE OF CONTENTS

INTRODUCTION

Welcome to "Communication Mastery: 42 Techniques for Workplace Success," where the art of conversation meets the science of connectivity. Imagine a toolbox, each drawer brimming with polished instruments, ready to tackle any communicative task from commanding a boardroom to drafting a compelling email. This book is designed to be that toolbox for your career.

Communication is the heartbeat of any thriving professional environment. It is the golden thread weaving through the tapestry of relationships, professional development, and, ultimately, career success. As you embark on this journey through the pages of this book, each chapter serves as a stepping-stone to mastering the nuances of effective communication.

The Chapters at a Glance

Let's peek at what lies ahead:

- **Active Listening**: Train your ears to be as effective as your voice. Tune in to understand, rather than just respond.

- **Articulation and Clarity**: Sharpen your ability to express ideas crisply, cutting through the noise like a hot knife through butter.

- **Non-Verbal Communication**: Decipher the unspoken language that often speaks louder than words.

- **Empathy**: Unlock the superpower of connecting with colleagues on a profound, emotional level.

- **Feedback**: Navigate the delicate art of giving and receiving insightful feedback to foster growth.

- **Emotional Intelligence**: Cultivate a keen awareness of your own emotions and those of others to communicate with finesse.

- ... and many more!

Each chapter will blend expertise with real-world scenarios, case studies, and a dash of storytelling charm.

Why This Book Matters

In my 20-plus years within the communication sphere, I've seen brilliant ideas wither due to poorly crafted messages and saw lackluster proposals win the day through persuasive delivery. Success isn't just about what you communicate; it's *how* you communicate it. Hence, every chapter of this book is crafted to be:

- **Engaging**: Expect engaging illustrations, relatable anecdotes, and a sprinkle of humor to keep you nodding along.

- **Practical**: Actionable advice will be at the heart of every chapter, ready for you to implement in your daily interactions.

- **Fact-based**: Rest easy, as every technique is grounded in rigorous research and real-life application.

- **Clear and Concise**: We've kept the jargon to a minimum. After all, clear water allows for a deep dive.

Taking the First Step

As you venture into the first chapter, remember that no technique is a panacea. It's the combination of methods, the sequence of strategies, and the adaptability of the approach that create the communication maestro. Whether you're a fresh intern, a mid-level manager, or a seasoned CEO, honing the craft of communication is an endless journey, and this book is here to escort you to your next destination.

So buckle up, and let's begin this expedition to the pinnacle of effective communication and workplace success.

ACTIVE LISTENING: THE FOUNDATION OF EFFECTIVE COMMUNICATION

The Key Ideas

Active listening is an essential skill for effective communication. It involves fully concentrating on the speaker, understanding their message, responding thoughtfully, and remembering what was said. Here are key ideas to grasp:

• **Full Attention**: Give the speaker your undivided attention. This means setting aside distracting thoughts and behaviors.

• **Non-Verbal Signals**: Your body language should show you are engaged. Nod occasionally, maintain eye contact, and lean forward slightly.

• **Avoid Interrupting**: Let the speaker finish their points before you speak. Interrupting disrupts the flow and conveys a lack of respect.

• **Reflecting and Clarifying**: Paraphrase the speaker's words and ask clarifying questions to ensure understanding.

• **Empathy**: Try to understand the speaker's perspective, even if it differs from your own.

• **Avoid Preparing a Rebuttal**: Listen to understand, not to reply.

Practical Implementation

To turn the concept of active listening into a skill you use daily, follow these steps:

1. **Minimize External Distractions**: Work in a quiet environment or use tools to reduce noise and interruptions.

2. **Engage with the Speaker**: Use prompts like "I see" or "Go on" to show your engagement without leading the conversation.

3. **Take Notes**: In appropriate situations, jot down key points, but don't let note-taking distract you.

4. **Practice**: Like any skill, active listening gets better with practice. Set daily goals to engage in active listening.

Use these strategies to show genuine interest and to enhance your active listening abilities:

• Similarly, maintain an open mind.

• Validate the speaker's points: "That makes sense because…"

• Encourage them by summarizing their key points at the end of the conversation.

Consistency and Evaluation

Developing active listening skills requires consistent practice and evaluation. Implement these habits into your daily communication:

• *Daily Check-ins*: At the end of each day, reflect on your conversations. Were you an active listener?

• *Feedback*: Ask colleagues or friends for feedback on your listening skills.

• *Set Specific Goals*: For example, aim to ask at least two clarifying questions in each meeting.

• *Observe Others*: Learn by watching skilled communicators in action.

Evaluate Progress: Assess your active listening skills regularly.

• Have your conversations become more productive?

• Do people seem more inclined to confide in you?

• Are you better at resolving conflicts?

In conclusion, active listening is not merely about quieting your own thoughts to let others speak; it's about deeply engaging with people to foster better understanding and relationships. Remember, effective communicators are not born — they're made through practice, patience, and an open heart.

ARTICULATING YOUR IDEAS: CLARITY AND PRECISION

The Key Ideas

Achieving clarity and precision in communication is paramount to ensure your ideas resonate and are understood by your audience.

- **Define Key Terms**: Begin by explicitly defining any jargon or technical terms. Limit their use to when they add genuine value.

- **Use Simple Language**: Opt for simple, straightforward words that make your message accessible to a broader audience.

- **Be Concise**: Deliver your message with as few words as necessary. Brevity underscores clarity.

- **Use Active Voice**: Active voice provides directness to your statements, making your ideas more engaging.

- **Organize Your Thoughts**: Structure your message. Start with the main idea, followed by supporting information.

- **Know Your Audience**: Tailor your message to the audience's level of understanding and interest.

Practical Implementation

Adopt a purposeful approach to make your communication unmistakably clear and precise.

1. **Create an Outline**: Start with a bullet-point outline to structure your ideas coherently.

2. **One Idea per Paragraph**: Stick to one main idea in each paragraph to maintain focus and clarity.

3. **Use Visuals**: Where possible, complement your points with diagrams or charts to enhance understanding.

4. **Practice Paraphrasing**: If a concept isn't understood initially, have an alternative explanation ready.

5. **Eliminate Fillers and Jargon**: Scrutinize your text for unnecessary words or industry-specific jargon that could confuse.

6. **Use Examples**: Concrete examples can often illustrate abstract ideas more clearly than lengthy descriptions.

Consistency and Evaluation

Maintaining a consistent approach in communication and regularly evaluating your methods are essential for continuous improvement.

- **Be Consistent**: Use the same terms throughout your communication to avoid confusion.

- **Seek Feedback**: Ask your audience if they understood your message and encourage them to ask questions.

- **Refine Your Message**: Use feedback to refine your approach for greater clarity.

- **Record Yourself**: Listening to how you communicate can offer insights into areas for improvement.

- **Practice**: Frequent articulation of complex ideas will help to hone your skills over time.

- **Peer Review**: Having peers evaluate your communication can provide a fresh perspective and valuable insights.

By integrating these methods into your daily communication, you can ensure that your ideas are received as intended—clear, precise, and impactful.

NON-VERBAL COMMUNICATION: READING BEYOND WORDS

The Key Ideas

Non-verbal communication is a critical aspect of human interaction. It encompasses all the unspoken elements that convey meaning, such as body language, facial expressions, gestures, posture, and tone of voice. Mastering the art of reading these cues can enhance your understanding of others and improve your ability to communicate effectively.

Recognize the Universality of Non-Verbal Signals

• Facial expressions for emotions like happiness, sadness, anger, and fear are universal.

• Gestures such as nodding for 'yes' and shaking the head for 'no' are common, though they can vary by culture.

Understand the Subtleties of Body Language

• Open body gestures generally signal availability and interest.

• Crossed arms might indicate defensiveness or resistance.

• Posture can denote confidence or lack thereof.

Interpret Paralinguistic Features

• Tone, pitch, and rate of speech provide insight into a speaker's emotional state.

• Pauses can emphasize importance or signal hesitation.

Context Is Crucial

• Non-verbal cues must be read in context; what is appropriate in one setting may not be in another.

• Cultural norms heavily influence non-verbal communication.

Recognize the Role of Personal Space

• Proxemics, or the use of space in communication, varies among individuals and cultures.

• Awareness of personal comfort zones can prevent discomfort or offense.

Practical Implementation

To utilize non-verbal communication effectively, practice these strategies:

1. **Observe Before Reacting**

   ○ Take a moment to absorb the whole scene and the non-verbal cues being offered.

2. **Mirror and Match**

   ○ Subtly mimic the body language of those you're interacting with to build rapport.

3. **Maintain Appropriate Eye Contact**

   ○ Eye contact can convey sincerity and interest, but be mindful not to stare.

4. **Be Mindful of Gestures**

   ○ Use gestures deliberately to emphasize or clarify your verbal communication.

5. **Stay Congruent**

   ○ Ensure your verbal and non-verbal messages are aligned for clear communication.

6. **Develop Empathy**

   ○ Try to understand the emotions behind non-verbal signals to respond more effectively.

Consistency and Evaluation

To improve your non-verbal communication skills:

• **Consistently Practice**: Like any skill, non-verbal communication improves with practice.

• **Seek Feedback**: Ask close colleagues or friends to provide honest feedback on your non-verbal cues.

• **Reflect and Adapt**: After interactions, reflect on your non-verbal behavior and adapt as necessary.

• **Observe Masters**: Watch public speakers, leaders, and skilled communicators to see how they use non-verbal communication.

In conclusion, the ability to read beyond words is an invaluable asset in professional settings. By mastering non-verbal communication, you can enhance your interactions and relationships in the workplace, leading to greater success.

THE POWER OF EMPATHY: CONNECTING ON A DEEPER LEVEL

The Key Ideas

Empathy is the art of understanding and sharing the feelings of others. At its core, empathy allows you to see the world through someone else's eyes, fostering a profound connection. Here are the key ideas to harness this power:

- **Recognition of Emotions:** Acquire the ability to recognize emotions in others. Pay close attention to verbal cues and body language.

- **Active Listening:** Listen not just to respond, but to understand. Avoid interrupting and offer your full attention.

- **Vulnerability:** Share your own emotions openly. It builds trust and strengthens relationships.

- **Perspective-Taking:** Imagine yourself in someone else's situation. This isn't about agreeing; it's about understanding.

- **Non-judgment:** Approach each interaction without prejudice or preconceived notions. Keep an open mind to all perspectives.

- **Respect for Boundaries:** Understand and respect the limits of what others are comfortable sharing.

Practical Implementation

To embody the key ideas and incorporate empathy into your daily interactions, consider the following steps:

1. **Reflect on Your Perceptions:**

   ○ Take time to self-reflect. Identify any biases that may cloud your understanding of others.

   ○ Regularly assess how your emotions affect your interactions.

2. **Enhance Your Emotional Vocabulary:**

   ○ Build a rich emotional vocabulary to better express and recognize feelings.

   ○ Practice identifying and naming emotions in yourself and others.

3. **Hone Your Listening Skills:**

   ○ Dedicate time to listen—focus on the speaker without planning your response.

   ○ Use reflective statements to show understanding.

4. **Engage in Role-Reversal Scenarios:**

   ○ Regularly practice imagining situations from another person's perspective.

   ○ Participate in exercises that require you to defend a viewpoint different from your own.

5. **Stay Curious:**

   ○ Ask open-ended questions to encourage deeper conversation.

○ Seek to learn more about the experiences of others.

6. **Embrace Feedback:**

  ○ Invite others to share how they feel about your interactions.

  ○ Be open to constructive criticism and use it to improve your empathetic abilities.

Consistency and Evaluation

Progress in developing empathy is fundamentally about commitment and practice. Maintain a consistent effort to apply empathy in every interaction by:

• **Setting Empathic Goals:** Regularly set specific, measurable goals for empathetic behavior.

• **Reflecting on Interactions:** After conversations, take time to evaluate the level of empathy displayed.

• **Seeking Surrogate Feedback:** Occasionally, get insights from third parties about how empathetic you appear in social contexts.

Self-Evaluation Techniques:

• Keep a journal documenting instances where you applied empathy and the outcomes.

• Use a rating scale to measure your empathetic responses for self-assessment.

Peer Evaluation Techniques:

• Establish a trusted group of colleagues or friends to provide you with honest feedback on your empathetic interactions.

• Participate in empathy-building workshops or seminars where peer evaluation is part of the learning process.

Note: Regularly revisit your implementation strategies. Adapt and refine them as necessary to align with both your personal growth and professional development. Remember, empathy is about authentic connections, not checklists—stay genuine in your endeavor to connect on a deeper level.

CONSTRUCTIVE FEEDBACK: GIVING AND RECEIVING

The Key Ideas

Feedback is a powerful tool for personal and professional growth. Constructive feedback, when done skillfully, benefits both the giver and the receiver. The core principle of constructive feedback is about being specific, factual, and focused on improvement rather than criticism.

- **Specificity**: Your feedback should be clear and target specific behaviors or actions, not general character traits.

- **Positive Intent**: Always approach feedback with the intent to help the other person grow, not to demonstrate superiority or find fault.

- **Actionable**: Ensure the feedback you provide can lead to actionable steps for improvement. Vague comments do not lead to change.

- **Timeliness**: Offer feedback as close to the event in question as possible.

- **Empathy**: Remember to empathize with the receiver's feelings and consider their perspective.

- **Balance**: Aim for a balanced approach that acknowledges strengths while also addressing areas for growth.

Practical Implementation

To implement these key ideas in real-world scenarios, follow these steps:

1. **Prepare Your Thoughts**: Before you give feedback, take time to consider what you want to say and how to say it constructively.

2. **Choose the Right Environment**: Find a private and neutral space to deliver your feedback, free from distractions or undue stressors.

3. **Use "I" Statements**: Frame your feedback from your perspective to prevent defensiveness (e.g., "I noticed that..." rather than "You always...").

4. **Be Direct but Gentle**: Get to the point without being abrasive or sugarcoating the message.

5. **Listen Actively**: Make the feedback a two-way conversation. Listen to the receiver's response to ensure understanding and create a collaborative plan for improvement.

6. **Follow Up**: Set a time to revisit the feedback, discussing progress and any further support that may be needed.

Receiving Feedback:

When on the receiving end, use these strategies to gain the most value:

1. **Listen Fully**: Before responding, make sure to listen to the entire message without interrupting.

2. **Separate Self from Behavior**: Acknowledge that the feedback is about behavior, not your worth as a person.

3. **Ask for Clarification**: Don't hesitate to ask for examples if you need more understanding of the feedback provided.

4. **Create an Action Plan**: Decide what steps you can take to improve and be open to suggesting these to the feedback giver as well.

5. **Display Appreciation**: Regardless of the feedback's nature, express thanks for the investment in your growth.

Consistency and Evaluation

The power of feedback is harnessed through consistency and regular evaluation.

- **Set Regular Check-ins**: Schedule consistent sessions for giving and receiving feedback to foster an atmosphere of continual improvement.

- **Create a Feedback Log**: Keep track of feedback given and received, actions taken, and progress made to evaluate growth over time.

- **Encourage a Feedback Culture**: Advocate for an environment where feedback is normalized and viewed as a constructive tool within the workplace.

Consistency ensures that feedback becomes a continual process, not a one-off event, leading to sustained development. Evaluation allows for reflection on feedback effectiveness and modifying approaches as needed for maximum benefit.

EMOTIONAL INTELLIGENCE IN THE WORKPLACE

The Key Ideas

Emotional Intelligence (EI) is the ability to understand and manage your own emotions, and those of the people around you. In the workplace, EI is crucial for fostering effective collaboration, leadership, and cultivating a positive work environment.

Self-Awareness

Understand your emotions, strengths, weaknesses, values, and the impact of your actions on others. Self-awareness is the groundwork for all other components of EI.

- Keep a journal of emotional responses

- Reflect on emotional reactions and outcomes

- Seek feedback from peers and superiors

Self-Regulation

Control or redirect your disruptive emotions and adapt to changing circumstances.

- Practice techniques such as deep-breathing to stay calm

- Prepare for known stress triggers in advance

- Set a clear standard for ethical conduct

Motivation

Harness your emotions to pursue goals with energy and persistence.

- Set personal performance benchmarks

- Celebrate small successes en route to larger goals

- Remain optimistic even when faced with failure

Empathy

Understand the emotions of others and respond appropriately. This skill is essential for individuals in leadership and client-facing roles.

- Actively listen to others without interrupting

- Observe body language for non-verbal cues

- Engage in perspective-taking exercises

Social Skills

Manage relationships, inspire others, and induce desirable responses.

- Develop communication that is clear and courteous

- Work cooperatively within a team environment

- Understand and navigate social complexities

Practical Implementation

Self-Assessment: Start by evaluating your current EI capabilities. Identify areas for improvement and set specific, measurable goals.

Mindfulness and Reflection: Regularly practice mindfulness to enhance your self-awareness. Reflect on your interactions and their outcomes.

Development Plans: Create a structured plan that includes learning opportunities such as workshops, mentorship, or coaching.

Workplace Culture: Cultivate an environment that encourages open communication, conflict resolution, and mutual support.

- Integrate team-building activities that highlight empathetic communication

- Host regular feedback sessions to facilitate understanding among colleagues

- Promote professional development focused on EI skills

Consistency and Evaluation

Consistency is paramount. Practicing EI skills should be a daily effort. Create routines and rituals that embed these practices into your work life.

- Schedule time for self-reflection

- Regularly check-in with team members on an emotional level

- Uphold ethical standards without compromise

Evaluation should be both internal and through external feedback. Incorporate regular self-evaluations as well as 360-degree feedback mechanisms to gauge your improvement.

- Use surveys or EI assessment tools to measure progress

- Set regular review points with your mentor or coach

- Adjust goals and strategies based on feedback

In conclusion, Emotional Intelligence in the workplace isn't a luxury, it's a necessity for success. It empowers you and those around you to work effectively and harmoniously, creating a resilient and vibrant work culture.

PUBLIC SPEAKING: CAPTIVATING YOUR AUDIENCE

The Key Ideas

Public speaking is not just about delivering a message; it's about engaging and moving an audience. Success comes from understanding the audience's needs, connecting with them on a personal level, and delivering a clear, memorable message. Here are the central tenets to captivate your audience:

1. **Know Your Audience**: Tailor your content to their interests, knowledge level, and needs. The more relatable your message, the more engaged they will be.

2. **Start Strong**: Open with a compelling statement, story, or question that piques interest immediately.

3. **Be Authentic**: Authenticity resonates. Speak honestly and from the heart.

4. **Clarity Is King**: Ensure your message is simple and focused. Avoid jargon and complex language.

5. **Visuals Aid Understanding**: Use visuals sparingly and effectively to complement your message.

6. **Body Language Matters**: Nonverbal cues can enhance or detract from your message. Use gestures and movement to reinforce your words.

7. **Vocal Variety**: Change your pitch, tone, and volume to maintain interest and emphasize key points.

8. **Interactive Engagement**: Involve your audience through questions, activities, or discussions to create a dynamic exchange.

9. **Conclude with Impact**: Leave your audience with a strong, actionable takeaway or thought-provoking message.

Practical Implementation

Putting the key ideas into practice requires preparation and skill development:

- **Audience Analysis**: Prior to your speech, gather information about your audience. Use surveys, social media, or direct engagement to know them better.

- **Rehearsing**: Practice your speech several times. Record yourself to analyze your performance and make necessary improvements.

- **Feedback Loops**: Engage friends, family, or colleagues for feedback on your content and delivery before the actual event.

- **Customizing Visuals**: Design slides or visual aids that are clear and not text-heavy. Visuals should support your message, not distract from it.

- **Master Nonverbal Communication**: Work on your facial expressions, eye contact, posture, and gestures. They should all be natural and convey confidence.

- **Voice Modulation Exercises**: Implement vocal warm-ups and exercises to improve articulation, projection, and expression.

- **Interactive Elements**: Plan out how you'll involve your audience. Will it be through direct questions, show of hands, or small group discussions?

- **Memorable Closing**: Craft your concluding statements carefully. They should encapsulate the essence of your talk and motivate your audience to think or act.

Consistency and Evaluation

To consistently captivate an audience, seek continuous improvement through evaluation and adaptation:

1. **Gather Feedback**: Use post-speech surveys, direct audience interaction, or professional critiques to get opinions on your performance.

2. **Self-Assessment**: Reflect on your own perceptions of the speech. What worked? What didn't?

3. **Peer Review**: If possible, have a trusted peer review your speech and delivery, providing an external perspective.

4. **Continuous Learning**: Stay informed on the latest best practices in public speaking, storytelling, and audience engagement. Regularly update your techniques.

5. **Adapt and Adjust**: Incorporate feedback into future speeches. Be willing to change your approach based on what you've learned.

Remember, captivating your audience isn't a one-time achievement; it's an ongoing process of honing your skills and adapting to each new group of listeners. With diligence and practice, the art of public speaking can become a compelling tool in your communication arsenal.

CONFLICT RESOLUTION: STRATEGIES FOR A HARMONIOUS WORKPLACE

The Key Ideas

Conflict in the workplace is inevitable. Diverse backgrounds, differing viewpoints, and stress can all lead to friction. Effective conflict resolution is critical not just for peace, but for productivity and employee satisfaction.

- **Identify the Conflict Early**: Recognize the warning signs – frustration, withdrawal, or outspoken discontent.

- **Encourage Open Communication**: Foster an environment where employees feel safe sharing their viewpoints.

- **Seek to Understand All Sides**: Before resolving, fully understand the perspectives involved.

- **Focus on the Issue, Not the Person**: Personal attacks escalate conflicts; keep discussions on the problems at hand.

- **Solution-Oriented Mindset**: Emphasize finding a resolution that benefits the workplace as a whole.

Practical Implementation

Combatting conflict requires a tactical approach. Here's how:

1. **Open Forums for Discussion**: Regularly scheduled meetings for airing concerns and discussing potential friction points can prevent escalation.

2. **Conflict Resolution Training**: Equip your team with the skills to handle disputes through professional development sessions.

3. **Mediation Process**: Establish a step-by-step process for mediating disputes that includes impartiality and confidentiality.

4. **Lead by Example**: Demonstrate collaborative behavior as a leader.

5. **Develop a Conflict Resolution Policy**: Document clear procedures and policies for how conflicts should be managed.

You can't predict every dispute, but you can create a robust framework for dealing with them.

Quick Tips for In-the-Moment Conflict Management:

• Stay calm and composed, no matter the situation.

• Listen actively and acknowledge the feelings and views expressed.

• Maintain a neutral stance while facilitating the discussion.

• Encourage empathy by asking parties to consider each other's perspectives.

Consistency and Evaluation

Consistent Practice:

- Regular training refreshers.

- Periodic reviews of the conflict resolution policy.

- Continuous support for open communication.

Evaluation:

- **Measuring the Outcomes**: Taking note of how quickly conflicts are resolved and the satisfaction level of the involved parties post-resolution.

- **Feedback Mechanisms**: Anonymous surveys to understand the effectiveness of the conflict resolution approach.

- **Adjustments and Adaptations**: Tailoring the conflict resolution strategies based on feedback and outcomes.

Balancing the scales of consistency and adaptability ensures your strategies remain effective over time. Remember, the goal is a dynamic, harmonious workplace.

PERSUASIVE COMMUNICATION: INFLUENCING WITH INTEGRITY

The Key Ideas

Persuasion is an art and a skill pivotal to communication, particularly in professional settings where your capacity to influence may shape outcomes significantly. It must be practiced with integrity, ensuring that your influence strengthens relationships, not undermines them.

Listen Actively: Genuine persuasion begins with listening. Understand others' perspectives, needs, and challenges.

Build Rapport: Establishing common ground creates a sense of trust and openness.

Clear Messaging: Be concise and articulate your point with clarity. Avoid jargon and speak in terms of benefits to the listener.

Evidence and Reasoning: Support your arguments with data, examples, and logical reasoning to establish credibility.

Emotional Appeal: Connect on an emotional level by tapping into the listener's values and emotions.

Ethical Influence: Stay true to your values and respect others' rights to have differing views.

Practical Implementation

- **Understand Your Audience:** Tailor your approach to their interests, beliefs, and preferred communication styles.

- **Set Clear Objectives:** Know what you want to achieve with your communication.

- **Structure Your Message:** Start with a strong opening, present your case, and conclude with a call to action.

- **Use Storytelling:** A relatable story can be more persuasive than statistics.

- **Engage With Questions:** Encourage dialogue to involve your audience in the conversation.

- **Be Patient:** Persuasion is sometimes a gradual process. Respect the time others may need to consider your perspective.

Consistency and Evaluation

Follow-Up: Reiterate key points through different communication channels to reinforce your message.

Seek Feedback: Regularly ask for and evaluate feedback to understand how your message is being received.

Adapt and Adjust: Be willing to refine your approach based on feedback and changing circumstances.

Maintaining consistency in your persuasive efforts while constantly evaluating and refining your approach will enhance your ability to influence effectively and with integrity.

Remember, the most persuasive communicators are not only influential, but they also prioritize ethical standards and mutual respect in every interaction.

PROFESSIONAL EMAIL ETIQUETTE

The Key Ideas

Email remains a cornerstone in professional communication. Mastering email etiquette can enhance your reputation and effectiveness. Here are the core principles:

Subject Lines Matter: Convey the purpose of your email succinctly. A clear subject line sets expectations and helps recipients prioritize your message.

Use Proper Salutations: Address recipients appropriately. For first-time communications, use more formal greetings. As relationships develop, you may adopt a less formal tone, if appropriate.

Be Clear and Concise: Time is precious. Keep your emails brief and to the point. Ensure your message is easily digestible at a glance.

Mind Your Tone: Without non-verbal cues, written language can be misinterpreted. Strive for a professional tone that is polite and considerate.

Proofread: Eliminating spelling or grammatical errors shows attention to detail and professionalism.

Professional Sign-off: Close your email with a suitable sign-off and your full name, position, and contact information.

Practical Implementation

Incorporate these strategies into your daily email practice:

1. Start with a checklist for email components: subject line, greeting, body, closing, and signature.

2. Draft your email and then revise, aiming for clarity and brevity.

3. Use bullet points or numbered lists to present multiple points or steps.

4. Read your email aloud to check tone and flow.

5. Set up a professional signature template in your email settings for consistent use.

Emphasize the importance of responding in a timely manner. Delayed responses can hinder productivity and relationships.

Consistency and Evaluation

To maintain professionalism, consistency in your email communications is key. Create personal guidelines or a reference document to ensure you adhere to best practices with every email.

Regularly evaluate your email habits:

• Track response times and aim for improvement.

• Request feedback from coworkers or mentors on your communication style.

• Stay updated on email communication trends and adjust your practices accordingly.

Implementing these strategies ensures you communicate effectively, project professionalism, and foster positive relationships through your email correspondence.

MASTERING THE ART OF STORYTELLING IN BUSINESS

The Key Ideas

Storytelling is a powerful tool in business communication, capable of engaging audiences, illustrating complex ideas, and influencing decision-making processes.

- **Human Connection**: Stories build bridges between the teller and the listener, creating a shared experience that fosters empathy and understanding.

- **Simplification of Complex Ideas**: A well-told story can distill intricate concepts into digestible narratives that are easier for audiences to comprehend.

- **Memory Enhancement**: People recall stories more easily than facts or figures due to their emotional resonance and narrative structure.

- **Persuasion and Influence**: Stories can subtly convey messages and values, persuading listeners without a hard sell approach.

Practical Implementation

- **Know Your Audience**: Tailor your story to match your audience's interests, experiences, and level of understanding.

- **Define the Core Message**: Identify the key takeaway you want your audience to remember and center your story around it.

- **Structure Your Story**: Outline a clear beginning, middle, and end. Ensure the story flows logically towards the desired conclusion.

- **Be Authentic**: Share genuine stories that reflect real experiences or well-researched scenarios to establish credibility.

- **Employ Vivid Imagery**: Use descriptive language to create visual scenes in the minds of your listeners.

- **Practice Delivery**: A story's impact is partly in the telling. Rehearse your pacing, tone, and body language to enhance the narrative.

- **Incorporate Data Mindfully**: While stories appeal to emotions, including relevant data can add credibility. Use data sparingly and effectively within the narrative.

Consistency and Evaluation

- **Regular Storytelling**: Integrate storytelling into your regular communication efforts to cultivate a consistent narrative around your business and values.

- **Feedback Loops**: Seek constructive feedback on your storytelling to understand the impact and areas for improvement.

- **Measure Outcomes**: Evaluate the effectiveness of your storytelling by monitoring audience engagement, recall, and subsequent actions.

Use storytelling as a strategic business tool to connect, engage, and influence with clarity and impact.

BUILDING TRUST: THE KEY TO LASTING RELATIONSHIPS

The Key Ideas

Trust is the cornerstone of any successful professional relationship. It's the foundation that supports collaboration, effective communication, and mutual respect.

1. **Transparency**: Honesty is your ally. Sharing information openly can prevent misunderstandings and demonstrate integrity.

2. **Reliability**: Do what you say you will do. Consistency in your actions builds confidence in your dependability.

3. **Empathy**: Understand others' perspectives. This demonstrates respect and can deepen connections.

4. **Competence**: Show your capability and knowledge. Delivering quality work establishes your credibility.

Practical Implementation

To turn these concepts into actionable steps, consider the following:

- **Communicate Clearly and Regularly**: Use simple language and verify understanding. Keep everyone informed about project statuses, changes, and decisions.

- **Set Expectations**: Define roles, responsibilities, and deadlines. Clarify goals upfront to avoid confusion.

- **Be Responsive**: React promptly to emails, calls, and requests. This signals respect for others' time and contributions.

- **Acknowledge and Address Issues**: Confront challenges directly and constructively. This approach can prevent escalation and promote problem-solving.

- **Ask for Feedback**: Invite input on your performance and be open to constructive criticism. This shows a commitment to personal growth and improvement.

Consistency and Evaluation

Consistency is about repeated, reliable behavior over time.

- Schedule regular check-ins with colleagues and teams to ensure alignment and address any trust issues.

- Reflect on feedback received and make necessary adjustments. Celebrate successes that result from trust-building.

Build trust with patience and diligence. Consider trust as an ongoing investment in your professional relationships, not as a one-off achievement. Regular self-evaluation and adaptation of your approach can lead to ever-stronger relationships.

THE ROLE OF HUMOR: WHEN AND HOW TO USE IT

The Key Ideas

Humor is a potent tool in communication. It can break the ice, forge connections, and defuse tension. The key to employing humor effectively is to understand its role and the context in which it's used. Here are the key ideas to grasp:

• **Appropriateness**: Humor must fit the situation and the audience. It should never offend or exclude.

• **Timing**: Well-timed humor can enhance a message, while poorly-timed can distract or even hurt.

• **Self-deprecation**: Laughing at oneself can show approachability and humility.

• **Understanding boundaries**: While some topics are generally safe, others can be sensitive. Know where to draw the line.

• **Purpose**: Use humor to add value, not just to get a laugh. It should support your communication goals.

Practical Implementation

To introduce humor into your communication with finesse, consider the following strategies:

- **Study Comedians**: Observe professionals. Notice how they pace their jokes and handle different audiences.

- **Start Small**: Introduce light humor with anecdotes or observations that relate to your topic.

- **Audience Analysis**: Understand who you're talking to and what might resonate with them.

- **Relevance is Key**: Make sure your humor is related to the topic at hand to reinforce your message, not detract from it.

- **Practice**: Like any skill, the more you practice humor, the better you'll become at judging when it's appropriate to use.

Examples:

1. During a tense meeting, a humorous remark related to the situation can lighten the mood.

2. Sharing a relevant comic strip or meme can serve as a visual and entertaining break during a presentation.

3. Telling a self-effacing story can make you more relatable and break down barriers.

Consistency and Evaluation

Regularly incorporating humor in your communication will help you become more comfortable with it and understand its effects. Evaluate your attempts at humor by:

- **Collecting Feedback**: Ask colleagues for their honest reactions to your use of humor.

- **Observing Reactions**: Pay attention to whether it brought smiles and engagement or if it fell flat.

- **Reflecting on Context**: Review the situation and determine if humor was appropriate or if it could have been misinterpreted.

- **Adjusting Accordingly**: If humor wasn't received well, reflect on the why and how, and adjust your future attempts.

Maintaining a light-hearted, approachable demeanor consistently will help establish your use of humor as a natural part of your interaction style in the workplace.

In conclusion, when used judiciously, humor can be a powerful tool in enhancing communication, building relationships, and easing workplace tension. It's important to understand the nuances of humor to ensure it's both effective and appropriate for your audience.

EFFECTIVE COMMUNICATION IN VIRTUAL TEAMS

The Key Ideas

Virtual teams are becoming the norm in the modern workplace, making effective communication an essential competency. To navigate this landscape, it's vital to understand the unique challenges and opportunities it presents. Unlike traditional in-person teams, virtual teams depend heavily on technology for interaction, which can lead to a lack of non-verbal cues, sometimes resulting in miscommunication.

Clarity is non-negotiable. Each message should be straightforward, leaving no room for ambiguity. Assume nothing —explain everything necessary for a full understanding of the task or message.

Responsiveness sets the tone for collaboration. Timely replies and feedback not only keep projects moving but also build trust among team members.

Cultural sensitivity is paramount. Virtual teams often cross time zones and cultural boundaries. Recognize and respect these differences to foster inclusivity and harmony.

Embrace technology, but don't let it overshadow humanity. Employ various tools for different communication needs, yet never forget the human element. Regular video calls can retain the personal touch that's often missing in emails and text chats.

Practical Implementation

1. **Choose the right tools.**

   ○ Use a reliable platform for video conferencing, such as Zoom or Skype.

   ○ Employ project management software like Trello or Asana for task tracking.

   ○ Leverage instant messaging apps like Slack or Microsoft Teams for quick, informal communication.

2. **Establish rules of engagement.**

   ○ Create a communication charter detailing preferred methods, frequency, and expected response times.

   ○ Decide on clear protocols for updating work status and sharing information.

3. **Adopt an agile communication style.**

   ○ Adjust your communication approach based on the context and needs of team members.

   ○ Use bullet points for concise updates, and expand on details during video calls or in longer emails.

4. **Foster team rapport.**

   ○ Initiate virtual team-building activities.

   ○ Encourage team members to share personal updates to build connections beyond work.

5. **Conduct effective virtual meetings.**

   ○ Circulate an agenda beforehand.

   ○ Keep meetings focused and within the scheduled time.

   ○ Ensure everyone has a chance to contribute.

6. **Promote active listening.**

   ○ Paraphrase or summarize what others say to confirm understanding.

   ○ Ask clarifying questions when in doubt.

7. **Prioritize written communication skills.**

   ○ Use simple, clear language.

   ○ Proofread messages to avoid misunderstandings.

8. **Maintain transparency and over-communicate when necessary.**

   ○ Regularly share updates on progress and changes.

Consistency and Evaluation

Institute regular check-ins. Weekly or bi-weekly meetings can ensure everyone is on the same page and provide a forum for feedback.

Track and measure communication effectiveness. Use surveys to gather team feedback on communication processes. Analyze response times, message clarity, and the frequency of misunderstandings to identify areas for improvement.

Iterate and adapt. Communication strategies should evolve as the team and organizational goals change. Encourage an open dialogue about what is working and where gaps exist.

In conclusion, mastering effective communication in virtual teams requires an intentional approach and a willingness to adapt. By setting clear expectations, staying responsive, and valuing transparency, virtual teams can overcome the barriers of distance and technology to achieve their collective goals.

COMMUNICATING ACROSS CULTURES: DIVERSITY AND INCLUSION

The Key Ideas

Understanding and embracing cultural diversity are core to effective communication in today's globalized world. Recognizing how customs, communication styles, and beliefs differ across cultures can help prevent miscommunication and foster inclusive environments. Here, we explore how:

- **Awareness is the Bedrock**: Know your own cultural biases and perceptions. Research and learn about other cultures, especially those you frequently interact with.

- **Active Listening Redefined**: Tune into verbal and non-verbal cues. Often, what's unspoken carries more weight in some cultures.

- **Language Matters**: Words can have different connotations in different cultures. Clarify and paraphrase to ensure understanding.

- **Humility is Key**: Approach differences with a learner's humility. Be ready to admit gaps in your knowledge and correct them.

- **Inclusivity is Non-Negotiable**: Create settings where all voices are heard and respected. This means adapting meetings and communications to be culturally sensitive.

- **Feedback Loops**: Encourage and establish open, regular feedback mechanisms that bridge the cultural divide.

Practical Implementation

Implementing effective cross-cultural communication strategies involves:

1. **Cultural Training**: Provide cross-cultural training workshops for all employees. Cover topics like cultural norms, etiquette, and values.

2. **Diverse Teams**: Build teams with cultural diversity in mind. It enhances perspective and fosters innovation.

3. **Language Support**: Offer language learning assistance and use plain language to aid understanding.

4. **Cultural Celebrations**: Celebrate diverse holidays and practices. It shows recognition and respect.

5. **Mentorship Programs**: Pair employees from different cultural backgrounds to promote shared understanding.

6. **Culturally Adaptive Policies**: Ensure company policies reflect cultural sensitivity and inclusiveness.

Consistency and Evaluation

Consistent application and regular evaluation of these practices ensure they don't become one-off initiatives but part of the corporate culture.

- **Regular Check-Ins**: Hold frequent discussions about cultural issues and the effectiveness of diversity practices.

- **Surveys and Feedback Forms**: Use them to gauge employee sentiment and obtain suggestions for improvement.

- **Performance Metrics**: Include diversity and inclusion metrics in performance reviews.

- **Continuous Learning**: Encourage ongoing education on cultural competencies through seminars and e-learning courses.

- **Accountability Structures**: Establish clear accountability mechanisms for inclusivity goals.

In conclusion, effective cross-cultural communication is not a box-ticking exercise. It requires deliberate action, ongoing commitment, and a genuine desire to understand and include. The outcome is a cohesive, dynamic workplace where every individual has the opportunity to contribute fully.

CRITICAL THINKING AND COMMUNICATION: CONNECTING THE DOTS

The Key Ideas

Critical thinking and communication are inextricably linked. To convey your thoughts effectively, you must first clearly understand them. Here's how they connect:

- **Analytical approach**: Both require a methodical mindset. Ask relevant questions, spot patterns, and dissect arguments.

- **Clarity**: Good communication starts with clear thinking. Confused thoughts lead to muddled messages.

- **Persuasion**: Convincing someone demands a logical flow of ideas, something critical thinking sharpens.

- **Problem-solving**: Identifying and articulating a problem is a critical first step toward resolution.

Practical Implementation

To integrate critical thinking into your communication:

1. **Be a Listener**:

   ◦ Practice active listening.

- Feed the main points back to the speaker to confirm understanding.

2. **Question Assumptions**:

- Why do I think this?

- Could I be wrong?

3. **Structure Your Thoughts**:

- Use mind maps or outlines.

- Start with a central idea and branch out.

4. **Check for Biases**:

- Are your beliefs affecting your interpretation?

- Distinguish facts from opinions.

5. **Simplify**:

- Convey your message directly.

- Avoid jargon or overly complex terms where not necessary.

6. **Practice Empathy**:

- Consider the listener's perspective.

- Tailor the message to resonate with them.

7. **Seek Feedback**:

- Encourage others to critique your ideas.

- Adjust your message based on constructive criticism.

8. **Reflect**:

- After each conversation, take time to reflect on what went well and what didn't.

Remember, the goal is understanding, not winning an argument. Enhance your empathy, express yourself clearly, and make a habit of constructive feedback.

Consistency and Evaluation

Maintain consistency:

- **Routine Checks**: Regularly assess your thought process.

- **Keep Learning**: Stay updated with communication techniques and critical thinking strategies.

- **Embrace Mistakes**: View them as learning opportunities.

Evaluate by asking:

- Did I get my point across effectively?

- Was there a logical flow to the discussion?

- How did the other party respond?

In conclusion, polish your thinking to sharpen your words. Master these skills through continuous practice and reflection. Your competence will grow, and your messages will resonate more powerfully.

NEGOTIATION SKILLS FOR WIN-WIN OUTCOMES

The Key Ideas

Negotiation is an art that involves reaching an agreement where all parties feel they have gained value. To ensure a win-win outcome, focus on these key practices:

1. **Prepare Thoroughly**: Know your goals, the other party's goals, and the limits of the negotiation.

2. **Build Relationships**: Strive to establish rapport and trust. People negotiate more favorably with someone they like and respect.

3. **Listen Actively**: Encourage the other party to talk more. Listen to understand their needs, interests, and constraints.

4. **Communicate Clearly**: Be concise and articulate your points effectively without being aggressive.

5. **Seek Mutual Benefit**: Aim for solutions that offer gains to both sides. Use 'and' instead of 'but' to connect ideas.

6. **Manage Emotions**: Keep a level head. Don't let the negotiation become personal.

7. **Be Creative**: Think outside the box for solutions that may not be immediately apparent.

8. **Focus on Interests, Not Positions**: Understand underlying interests rather than getting stuck on stated positions.

9. **Know When to Walk Away**: Recognize the point where the negotiation no longer serves your interests.

Practical Implementation

Implementing these key ideas effectively involves certain tactics:

• **Prioritize Your Issues**: Rank the matters most important to you. Know what you can compromise on and what is non-negotiable.

• **Emphasize Collaboration**: Use language that underscores partnership, such as "How can we solve this together?"

• **Use Objective Criteria**: Base the negotiation on objective standards to avoid bias and facilitate fair resolution.

• **Develop Alternatives**: Have a well-thought-out Plan B (BATNA) if negotiations fail to produce an agreement.

• **Leverage Silence**: Sometimes, staying quiet can be powerful, forcing the other party to think or reveal more than they intended.

Consistency and Evaluation

Consistency in negotiations builds your reputation as a reliable partner. Evaluate your tactics after each negotiation:

• **Review the Process**: Analyze what worked, what didn't, and why.

• **Gather Feedback**: If possible, get insight from the other party about how they perceived the negotiation.

- **Refine Strategies**: Use this information to hone your approach for next time.

Remember, negotiation skills are improved over time through practice, reflection, and persistence. Stay committed to the principles of win-win negotiation, and your efforts will lead to better outcomes and stronger relationships.

BUILDING RAPPORT: THE LITTLE THINGS THAT MATTER

The Key Ideas

Building rapport is the cornerstone of successful communication. It's about making a connection that fosters trust, understanding, and mutual respect. To achieve this, focus on the subtleties of interaction that leave a lasting positive impression.

- **Active Listening**: Show genuine interest by nodding, maintaining eye contact, and avoiding interruptions. This demonstrates respect and attentiveness.

- **Mirroring**: Subtly mimic the other person's body language, tone, and expressions. It creates an unconscious bond, making them feel more at ease.

- **Positive Reinforcement**: Acknowledge what the other person says which validates their thoughts and encourages open sharing.

- **Small Gestures**: Remember names, shared experiences, and personal details. These indicate you value the relationship beyond its professional utility.

- **Consistency**: Be consistent in your behavior. People trust predictable patterns and it strengthens relationships over time.

• **Empathy**: Strive to understand the other person's perspective. Empathy builds deep connections and shows genuine care for their feelings and experiences.

Practical Implementation

To implement these ideas in your daily interactions:

1. Start conversations by asking about the other person's interests or recent experiences.

2. Listen more than you speak. Use prompts like "Tell me more" to delve deeper into their thoughts.

3. Use the person's name early and often in the conversation to create a personal connection.

4. Pay attention to non-verbal cues; they often reveal more than words.

5. Offer sincere compliments and show appreciation for their input.

6. Share small, relatable pieces of your own experiences to create common ground.

7. Always follow through on promises or commitments to show reliability.

Remember, rapport is built over time. These actions must be authentic and consistent for them to foster genuine connections.

Consistency and Evaluation

Maintaining **consistent efforts** in building rapport is crucial. Actions should not be one-off gestures but part of an ongoing effort to connect. Regular **self-evaluation** helps you remain genuine and improve interpersonal skills.

- Weekly, assess the quality of your interactions. Have you been actively listening and engaging?

- Reflect on the responses you receive. Are they warm and open, or short and disconnected?

- Adjust your approach as needed, remembering that different personalities may require different tactics.

In conclusion, rapport is nurtured through consistent, genuine, and empathetic engagement. It's not about grand gestures but the little things done regularly that weave the fabric of strong, lasting professional relationships.

MINDFUL COMMUNICATION: BEING PRESENT

The Key Ideas

Mindfulness, the practice of staying attuned to the current moment, enhances communication by focusing your attention. It's about listening actively and speaking with purpose. Here's why it matters:

- **Attention is a gift**: By being fully present, you show respect and value to the conversational partner.

- **Non-verbal cues**: Observing these offers deeper understanding. Mindfulness helps you detect them.

- **Reduces misunderstandings**: Being present minimizes distractions, clarifying both delivery and reception of messages.

- **Improves memory**: Fully engaging in the conversation helps recall the details later.

Practical Implementation

1. **Start with breath**: Take a few deep breaths before a conversation to center yourself.

2. **Eye contact**: Establish and maintain appropriate eye contact to stay engaged.

3. **Active listening**: Nod and provide verbal affirmations that you're following along.

4. **Silence your inner critic**: Reserve judgment and focus on understanding before responding.

5. **Clarify and summarize**: Echo back what's said to ensure you've understood it correctly.

6. **Be patient**: Allow the conversation to unfold naturally without rushing to fill silence.

7. **Single-task**: Avoid multitasking. Give the conversation your full attention.

8. **Technology off**: Turn off or silence notifications and other gadgets that could distract.

Consistency and Evaluation

To build a habit of mindful communication, integrate these techniques daily. Reflect regularly on your conversations. Ask yourself:

- Did I listen more than talk?

- Was I able to stay present throughout the discussion?

- How accurately could I recall details afterward?

Track which methods work best for you and tweak your approach accordingly. Mindful communication, like any skill, improves with practice and reflection.

TECHNOLOGY AND COMMUNICATION: TOOLS FOR THE MODERN WORKPLACE

The Key Ideas

Today's workplace is a dynamic environment driven by technology and the continuous evolution of communication tools. Understanding how to harness these tools is vital to enhancing productivity, collaboration, and engagement.

- **Select the Right Tools**: Assess the needs of your team to choose platforms that facilitate effective communication.

- **Embrace Mobility**: Utilize mobile-oriented communication apps to ensure connectivity and access to information anytime, anywhere.

- **Master Asynchronous Communication**: Leverage tools like email, project management software, and collaborative documents to enable team members to contribute on their own schedules.

- **Prioritize Cybersecurity**: Opt for communication tools with strong security measures to protect sensitive information.

- **Facilitate Real-Time Collaboration**: Employ video conferencing and live document editing tools to replicate in-person interactions.

Practical Implementation

1. **Introduce a Communication Hub**: Centralize conversations, tasks, and projects in one place with a platform like Slack or Microsoft Teams.

2. **Foster Digital Etiquette**: Establish clear guidelines on communication practices to maintain professionalism and respect.

3. **Use Video Conferencing Effectively**: Ensure video calls are productive with agendas, time limits, and post-meeting summaries.

4. **Leverage Chatbots for Routine Tasks**: Automate responses to common queries, freeing up time for more complex tasks.

5. **Encourage Regular Check-ins**: Use technology to maintain consistent communication rhythms, balancing the offer of flexibility.

Consistency and Evaluation

• **Set Benchmarks for Response Times**: Define expectations for different communication methods to avoid confusion and delays.

• **Track Communication Metrics**: Monitor email response times, number of messages, and engagement to identify areas for improvement.

• **Solicit Feedback**: Regularly ask team members about the effectiveness of communication tools and practices.

• **Review Tools Annually**: Stay current with emerging technologies to ensure you are using the best platforms available.

- **Adapt and Evolve**: Be agile and willing to adjust strategies based on team needs and technology advancements.

ADAPTING YOUR COMMUNICATION STYLE TO DIFFERENT PERSONALITIES

The Key Ideas

Adapting your communication style to different personalities is not about manipulation; it's about building better, more respectful relationships. **People often receive and process information differently based on their personality traits.** Recognizing and adjusting to these differences can lead to more effective and harmonious interactions.

- **Listen actively:** Before you can adapt your style, you need to understand the other person. This means listening more than you speak and paying attention to verbal and non-verbal cues.

- **Personality models:** Familiarize yourself with basic personality models (such as the Myers-Briggs Type Indicator or the Big Five personality traits) to help identify patterns in behaviors and preferences.

- **Flexibility is key:** Be willing to step out of your communication comfort zone. Your adaptability will often be reciprocated, leading to more productive exchanges.

- **Clarity over complexity:** Regardless of the personality type, your message should be clear. Don't sacrifice understanding for elaborate wording.

- **Empathy matters:** Empathizing with the other person's perspective can help you tailor your communication in a way that resonates with them.

Practical Implementation

Adjusting to the Introvert/Extrovert Spectrum:

- With introverts, give them time to reflect before expecting a response.

- Extroverts may appreciate a more energetic and interactive approach.

Dealing with Thinkers vs. Feelers:

- Thinkers often prefer data and facts.

- Feelers respond best to personal connections and emotional language.

Organizing for Judgers and Perceivers:

- Judgers value structure and decisiveness; offer clear options and conclusions.

- Perceivers like to keep their options open and explore; present information in a more flexible manner.

Communicating with Assertive vs. Agreeable Individuals:

- Assertive people respect directness and strength.

- Agreeable persons value harmony and diplomacy.

Adapting to Openness:

- Those high in openness enjoy novelty and complexity in conversations.

- A more conventional and straightforward approach may work well for those with lower openness scores.

Strategies for Implementing Adaptation:

1. **Observe:** Note the other person's preferred communication style in various contexts.

2. **Mirror:** Reflect their style to some extent. This doesn't mean mimicking but aligning with their energy and pace.

3. **Ask:** When in doubt, ask for feedback on your communication methods.

Consistency and Evaluation

Being consistent in your efforts to adapt your communication style is important for genuine relationships. It's not about a one-off adaptation, but a sustained effort to interact effectively.

• **Consistency:** Regularity in adapting your style helps reinforce trust.

• **Feedback loops:** Create opportunities for feedback to understand if your adaptation is effective.

• **Reflection:** Post-interaction, reflect on what worked and what didn't.

Remember, adapting your style is about becoming a versatile communicator, not about losing your authenticity.

Key takeaways:

• Adaptation enhances interactions but requires sincere effort.

• Regular evaluation and willingness to modify your approach is crucial.

• Effective communication often depends upon your ability to recognize and respect individual differences.

GROUP DYNAMICS AND TEAM COMMUNICATION

The Key Ideas

Group dynamics significantly affect workplace outcomes. Understanding how teams interact enables smoother communication, fosters inclusivity, and drives productivity. Here are the core ideas:

- **Roles and Responsibilities**: Define clear roles and ensure each member understands their responsibilities and the contribution expected from them. This gives a sense of purpose and minimizes conflict over work distribution.

- **Communication Channels**: Establish open and reliable channels for sharing information. This might include regular meetings, shared digital workspaces, or effective use of email and messaging.

- **Trust and Transparency**: Foster an environment where members feel comfortable expressing ideas and concerns. Trust is built through honesty, respecting confidentiality, and giving everyone a voice.

- **Feedback Culture**: Feedback should be constructive, specific, and intended to promote growth. It needs to be both given and received in the spirit of improvement.

- **Conflict Resolution**: Approach conflict as an opportunity for growth. Encourage active listening, empathy, and a focus on finding mutually beneficial solutions.

- **Common Goals**: Strengthen team bonds by establishing shared objectives. Teams with a clear, common direction are more cohesive and collaborative.

- **Diverse Perspectives**: Embrace different viewpoints as a resource. A team with varied experiences and skills is more innovative and adept at problem-solving.

Practical Implementation

Implement these strategies to improve team dynamics and communication:

1. **Regular Check-Ins**: Schedule consistent meetings for the team to align on goals and responsibilities and address any concerns. This can prevent misunderstandings and disconnection.

2. **Collaboration Tools**: Utilize project management software or collaboration platforms to keep everyone on the same page and streamline workflows.

3. **Role Clarification Exercises**: Run sessions to discuss and define team roles. Allow members to express what tasks energize them and align roles with strengths where possible.

4. **Team-building Activities**: Engage in activities outside of work tasks to build rapport and deepen trust among team members.

5. **Communication Training**: Invest in workshops or training sessions to improve interpersonal communication skills, focusing on active listening, nonverbal cues, and empathy.

6. **Conflict Role Play**: Simulate conflicts and role-play resolution scenarios to prepare the team for handling disputes effectively.

7. **Decision-Making Process**: Outline a clear process for making decisions that involve input from all levels, ensuring buy-in and reducing resistance.

8. **Recognition and Reward**: Celebrate team successes and acknowledge individual contributions to bolster morale and motivate continued excellence.

Consistency and Evaluation

To ensure the longevity of effective group dynamics and communication, maintain consistency in practices and regularly evaluate team function:

• **Regular Reviews**: Hold monthly or quarterly reviews to assess the effectiveness of communication and the health of team dynamics.

• **Surveys and Feedback Forms**: Use anonymous surveys to gauge team sentiment and receive candid feedback.

• **Adaptation and Growth**: Be willing to adapt strategies based on feedback and changing team needs. Continuous learning and development should be a priority.

• **Metrics and Objectives**: Set clear metrics for success that relate to communication and collaboration. Revisit them during evaluations to measure progress.

• **Mentorship Programs**: Pair less experienced team members with mentors to enhance communication skills and integration into the group.

In conclusion, effective group dynamics and team communication arise from structured practices, a culture of openness, and ongoing evaluation. Implement these principles with a commitment to adaptability, and watch your team thrive.

PERSONAL BRANDING: CRAFTING YOUR PROFESSIONAL NARRATIVE

The Key Ideas

Personal branding is the art of deliberately crafting and influencing how the public perceives you, presenting yourself in a way that makes your strengths and unique qualities stand out. It's a strategic presentation of your skills, experience, and personality in the professional world.

1. **Identify Your Unique Value Proposition**: Understand what sets you apart from others in your field. This could be a particular skill set, experience, or personal qualities that make you invaluable.

2. **Define Your Audience**: Know who you are trying to reach with your personal brand. This could be future employers, clients, or peers in your industry.

3. **Develop a Professional Narrative**: Your narrative is the story of your career and personal development. It should be compelling and reflect your professional path, achievements, and goals.

4. **Create a Consistent Image Across Platforms**: Your personal brand should translate seamlessly across different platforms, from LinkedIn to your personal website or blog.

5. **Communicate with Authenticity**: Authenticity builds trust. Be genuine in your interactions and when sharing content related to your brand.

6. **Maintain Professionalism**: Whether online or in-person, keep interactions professional. This reflects on your personal brand and can either reinforce or diminish your reputation.

Practical Implementation

To implement your personal brand strategy, follow these steps:

1. **Conduct a Self-Assessment**: Evaluate your strengths, weaknesses, achievements, and values. Reflect on what you have to offer that is distinctive.

2. **Set Clear Goals**: Outline what you want to achieve with your personal branding efforts. Whether it's a job promotion or becoming a thought leader in your field, your goals will direct your action plan.

3. **Build a Professional Profile**: Use professional photos and concise, impactful language to build your profiles on LinkedIn and other relevant platforms. Spotlight your unique value proposition.

4. **Content Creation**: Generate value by creating and sharing content that aligns with your brand. This elevates your status as a knowledgeable professional in your area of expertise.

5. **Networking**: Engage with others in your industry to build relationships and increase your visibility. Attend events, join forums, and connect with peers online.

6. **Feedback and Adaptation**: Seek constructive feedback on your personal brand and be willing to make adjustments to improve how you are perceived.

Consistency and Evaluation

Maintaining consistency is crucial to the strength of your personal brand.

- **Visual Identity**: Use a consistent profile picture and color scheme across all online platforms.

- **Voice and Tone**: Keep your communication style consistent, whether in writing or speaking.

- **Professional Conduct**: Ensure that your behavior is always professional and in line with your established personal brand.

Evaluate your brand regularly:

1. **Monitor Your Online Presence**: Check your social media profiles, Google yourself frequently, and gauge the public perception of your brand.

2. **Track Professional Goals**: After setting your goals, evaluate whether your personal branding efforts are helping you to meet them.

3. **Adjust as Needed**: Be ready to refine your approach based on feedback and the evolving circumstances of your career.

In conclusion, personal branding isn't about creating an idealized image of yourself, but rather about thoughtfully crafting and managing your professional narrative to align with your career objectives. Through consistent practice and regular evaluation, you ensure that your personal brand remains vibrant and effective.

NETWORKING: EFFECTIVE STRATEGIES FOR BUILDING CONNECTIONS

The Key Ideas

Networking is not just about expanding your professional contacts; it's about building meaningful relationships that can mutually benefit all parties involved. To accomplish this, consider the following principles:

- **Value Exchange:** Networking is a two-way street. Think about what you can offer to others, not just what they can provide you.

- **Authenticity:** Be genuine in your interactions. Authenticity builds trust, which is the cornerstone of any strong relationship.

- **Listening Skills:** Great networkers are great listeners. Show genuine interest in what others have to say.

- **Follow-Up:** After a connection is made, follow up. It shows that you value the relationship.

Practical Implementation

Putting these ideas into practice involves actionable steps:

1. **Target the Right Events**

   ○ Attend industry conferences, workshops, and seminars relevant to your field.

   ○ Participate in local community functions where like-minded professionals gather.

2. **Prepare Your Introduction**

   ○ Develop a concise and intriguing way to introduce yourself that includes your expertise and interests.

   ○ Practice your pitch but be ready to adapt it to the conversation.

3. **Ask Open-Ended Questions**

   ○ Initiate conversations by asking questions that require more than a yes or no answer.

   ○ Show interest in their work and experiences.

4. **Share Useful Information**

   ○ Offer insights or helpful resources related to the discussion.

   ○ Be a connector by introducing new contacts to other professionals when you see a potential synergy.

5. **Set Networking Goals**

   ○ Aim to make a certain number of quality connections rather than collecting as many business cards as possible.

   ○ Quality over quantity is key.

6. **Leverage Social Media**

   ○ Use platforms like LinkedIn to research potential contacts and to keep in touch after an initial meeting.

7. **Create a Follow-Up System**

   ○ Keep a record of whom you've met, key personal details you've learned, and when you last reached out.

   ○ Schedule regular times for following up with your contacts.

Consistency and Evaluation

For networking to be effective, it has to be consistent:

- **Routine Interaction**

  ○ Set aside dedicated time each week for networking activities.

  ○ Be consistent with your follow-up; don't let contacts go cold.

- **Evaluate Your Network**

  ○ Periodically assess the value of each connection.

  ○ Identify any gaps in your network where you might benefit from additional connections.

- **Refine Your Approach**

  ○ Reflect on what's working and what isn't.

  ○ Make adjustments to your strategy as needed to maintain and grow your network.

Remember, networking is about building lasting relationships. Take the time to invest in others, and they will likely invest in you.

Keep interactions meaningful and beneficial to all involved, and your network will become one of your greatest professional assets.

MANAGING UP: COMMUNICATION WITH SUPERIORS

The Key Ideas

Managing up involves effective communication and relationship-building with your bosses. Here are the core concepts:

- **Understand Their Communication Style:** Adapt to your superiors' preferred method and style of communication.

- **Set Clear Expectations:** Discuss and agree upon objectives, deadlines, and feedback processes.

- **Be Proactive:** Anticipate needs and offer solutions rather than waiting for instructions.

- **Build Trust:** Honesty and reliability in small tasks lead to trust in larger matters.

- **Focus on Results:** Prioritize tasks that align with your superior's goals and the organization's objectives.

Practical Implementation

To put these ideas into practice:

1. **Observe and Adapt:** Note how your boss communicates and mimic that style for better rapport.

2. **Schedule Regular Check-ins:** Propose consistent meetings to ensure alignment and display initiative.

3. **Prepare for Meetings:**

   ○ Bring a clear agenda.

   ○ Highlight completed tasks.

   ○ Have a list of items needing their input.

4. **Follow Through:** Deliver on promises and update proactively on progress or delays.

5. **Seek Feedback:** Encourage constructive criticism and show you can act on it.

Consistency and Evaluation

Remaining consistent in your managing up practices is vital. Regularly evaluate the effectiveness of your communication:

• Are you meeting the agreed-upon objectives?

• Has trust been established and is it growing?

• Is the feedback you're receiving mostly positive or are improvements needed?

Refine your strategies as needed. Remember, effective upward management enhances your professional growth and contributes positively to your work environment.

CRISIS COMMUNICATION: KEEPING COOL UNDER PRESSURE

The Key Ideas

Effective crisis communication is about maintaining control and clarity under intense scrutiny. Adopt these fundamental principles:

- **Swift Response**: Time is critical. Delay can exacerbate the crisis. Aim to communicate promptly to stakeholders.

- **Transparency**: Honesty builds trust. Be as open as possible without compromising sensitive information.

- **Preparation**: Have a crisis management plan with designated spokespersons and clear protocols.

- **Clarity**: Keep messages understandable. Avoid jargon, ambiguity, and overly complex explanations.

- **Empathy**: Recognize the impact on those affected. This humanizes the organization and facilitates connections.

- **Controlled Emotions**: Stay composed. Emotional responses can cloud judgment and escalate situations.

Practical Implementation

To put these principles into action, follow a structured approach:

1. **Initial Assessment**: Quickly gauge the situation's severity and potential impact. Determine who needs to be contacted first.

2. **Assemble the Team**: Activate your crisis management team immediately, ensuring all key players are present.

3. **Craft the Message**: Create a concise, clear statement that acknowledges the issue, expresses empathy, and outlines the next steps.

4. **Select Communication Channels**: Choose appropriate mediums—social media, press releases, emails—based on the situation and audience.

5. **Deliver Consistently**: Use consistent messaging across all platforms to avoid confusion and mixed messages.

6. **Monitor and Adapt**: Stay attuned to reactions and feedback. Be ready to adjust your approach as needed.

Remember to:

• Prioritize important information, breaking it down into digestible points.

• Avoid speculation and stick to verified facts.

• Establish a dedicated point of contact for ongoing inquiries.

Consistency and Evaluation

Maintain a consistent communication flow and regularly evaluate your crisis communication strategy:

- **Consistent Updates**: Keep stakeholders informed, even if the update is that there is no update.

- **Messaging Alignment**: Continually ensure all communications are aligned with your core message and current facts.

- **Feedback Loop**: Create channels for receiving real-time feedback to gauge the effectiveness of your communications.

- **Post-Crisis Analysis**: After the event, analyze the response to identify strengths and areas for improvement.

In crisis situations, effective communication can significantly influence outcomes. It's not merely about damage control; it's about demonstrating leadership and safeguarding your organization's reputation.

PROFESSIONAL WRITING: CRAFTSMANSHIP IN BUSINESS DOCUMENTS

The Key Ideas

Writing in a professional environment mandates clarity, conciseness, and a persuasive undertone that aligns with the established goals. Crafting impactful business documents requires an understanding of the core principles that drive effective communication.

- **Clarity** is paramount; your writing should convey messages unambiguously.

- **Conciseness** contributes to clarity by eliminating superfluous words or phrases.

- **Purpose-Driven Content**: Every document should have a defined objective.

- **Audience Awareness**: Tailoring your language and content to the reader's needs enhances receptiveness.

- **Professional Tone**: Maintain a formal yet accessible tone. Balance professionalism with approachability.

- **Structure and Format**: Employ a logical structure that guides the reader through your arguments seamlessly.

- **Visual elements**: Use lists, headings, and whitespace to promote ease of reading.

Practical Implementation

1. **Start with an Outline**: Before you write, plan. Lay out the main points you aim to cover.

2. **The First Draft**: Write down your ideas. Focus on content over form. Precision comes later.

3. **Review and Revise**: Iterate. Check for clarity, conciseness, and fluidity. Refine your arguments.

4. **Peer Review**: Whenever possible, a fresh pair of eyes can offer insightful feedback.

5. **Final Draft**: After incorporating feedback, polish your document for submission or distribution.

6. **Active Voice**: Use the active voice for more powerful sentences that are straightforward.

7. **Eliminating Jargon**: Cut technical terms when they aren't essential. Use simple language.

8. **Bullet Points and Lists**:

   - Are scannable.

   - Break information into digestible pieces.

   - Are effective for highlighting key points.

9. **Bold and Italics**: Use sparingly for emphasis only.

Consistency and Evaluation

Set and adhere to standards to ensure consistency across all written communications.

- **Style Guide Adherence**: Refer to a company-specific style guide or universally accepted guides (like AP or Chicago Manual of Style).

- **Regular Audits**: Evaluate your documents periodically. Ensure they still meet the set objectives and standards.

- **Feedback Mechanism**: Implement a system to gather feedback on your documents' effectiveness from peers and readers.

- **Continuous Improvement**: Adapt your writing practices based on feedback and new insights.

Remember, professional writing is not a static skill but a dynamic practice that evolves with experience and continual learning.

COACHING AND MENTORING: DEVELOPING OTHERS THROUGH DIALOGUE

The Key Ideas

Understand the Difference

- Coaching is task-oriented, short-term, performance-driven.

- Mentoring is relationship-oriented, long-term, development-focused.

Listening is Key

- Active listening is paramount. Hear what is said, and what's left unsaid.

- Use paraphrasing to ensure clarity and understanding.

Ask Powerful Questions

- Open-ended questions foster deeper reflection.

- Avoid leading questions that can bias the conversation.

Feedback Should Empower

- Provide balanced feedback: highlight strengths and pinpoint areas for growth.

- Ensure feedback is specific, timely, and actionable.

Goals Must Be SMART

- Specific, Measurable, Achievable, Relevant, Time-bound.

- Collaborate with the mentee/coachee to set these goals.

Encourage Self-Reflection

- Self-discovery promotes lasting change.

- Guide mentees to draw insights and conclusions independently.

Foster a Growth Mindset

- Emphasize learning from failures as much as from successes.

- Praise effort and resilience, not just outcomes.

Practical Implementation

Establish the Relationship

- Align on expectations and confidentiality from the outset.

- Build trust; it's the foundation of effective coaching and mentoring.

Dialoguing Techniques

- Utilize the GROW model: Goals, Reality, Options, Will.

- Use the CLEAR model: Contracting, Listening, Exploring, Action, Review.

Provide Resources

- Share articles, books, and connect them with networks.

- Offer tools for self-assessment and progress tracking.

Regular Check-ins

- Schedule consistent, dedicated time for discussions.
- These check-ins ensure accountability and support.

Consistency and Evaluation

Consistent Practice

- Regular coaching and mentoring embeds the learning process.
- Inconsistency can derail progress and undermine trust.

Monitor Progress

- Set milestones for development and review them regularly.
- Adapt plans based on progress, not emotions or assumptions.

Gather Feedback

- Solicit feedback on your approach to refine your methods.
- Use a 360-degree feedback system where appropriate.

Evaluate and Evolve

- Reflect on the effectiveness of dialogue strategies.
- Always be open to new techniques and adapt as necessary.

Document the Journey

- Keep records of the growth and changes.

• Celebrate successes with your mentee/coachee to motivate further development.

THE ART OF LISTENING: BEYOND THE BASICS

The Key Ideas

Active Listening
It's more than just hearing words. Engage with the speaker through nodding, eye contact, and brief verbal confirmations like "I see" or "Understood".

Empathetic Understanding
Put yourself in their shoes. It's not just about the content; grasp the speaker's emotions and perspective.

Non-Verbal Cues
Watch closely. Body language and tone can often tell more than words themselves.

Patience and Open-mindedness
Resist the urge to interrupt. Let the speaker complete their thoughts. Be receptive to new ideas, even if they challenge your beliefs.

Feedback
Clarify and confirm. Ask questions when necessary, and repeat key points to ensure mutual understanding.

Distraction Management
Create an environment conducive to listening. Minimize external interruptions and internal mental noise.

Remembering Details
Train your memory to capture and store information.

Practical Implementation

1. **Set the Stage**

   ○ Find a quiet, comfortable place for conversations.

   ○ Ensure good lighting and minimal distractions.

2. **Non-Verbal Engagement**

   ○ Maintain eye contact, without staring, to show attentiveness.

   ○ Use appropriate facial expressions and nods.

   ○ Keep your posture open and inviting.

3. **Verbal Techniques**

   ○ Encourage speakers with prompts like "Go on" or "And then?"

   ○ Paraphrase their points to show understanding: "*So, what you're saying is...*"

   ○ Reflect emotions: "You seem thrilled about the project."

4. **Question Effectively**

   ○ Ask open-ended questions to draw out more information.

   ○ Use closed questions for specifics: "Did you meet the deadline?"

   ○ Probe gently for depth without appearing intrusive.

5. **Practice Mindful Listening**

   ○ Focus fully on the speaker - no multitasking.

- Observe your thoughts but return your focus to the conversation.

6. **Memory Aids**

   - Summarize after every few sentences.

   - Jot down key points if appropriate.

   - Repeat names and crucial details to enhance retention.

Consistency and Evaluation

Establish a Routine To improve, integrate listening into your daily life. Practice in every conversation, whether it's a meeting or a casual chat.

Self-Assessment Regularly assess your listening skills:

- Did I understand the key points?

- Was my feedback helpful?

- Did I remain present throughout the conversation?

Seek Feedback Courageously ask others how well you listen. Take their observations seriously.

Reflect on Conversations After important discussions, take a moment to reflect. How effectively did you listen? How could you improve for next time?

Set Listening Goals Target specific improvements: 'Today I'll remember names,' or 'I'll avoid interrupting'

Stay Curious and Compassionate Embrace every conversation as an opportunity to learn, both the content and about the art of listening itself.

The art of listening is a dynamic skill. It demands practice, presence, and a genuine interest in the person speaking. It's about building stronger, more informed, and connected relationships. By mastering these techniques, you'll not only hear more, but you'll also be heard when it's your turn to speak.

TIME MANAGEMENT: BALANCING COMMUNICATION WITH PRODUCTIVITY

The Key Ideas

Time is your most valuable asset. Mastering its allocation is essential for achieving a harmonious balance between communication and productivity in the workplace. The core concept hinges on prioritizing tasks and setting boundaries to ensure focused work without neglecting interpersonal connections.

- **Prioritize Effectively**: Determine which tasks require immediate attention and which can be deferred. Use tools like the Eisenhower Matrix to categorize and prioritize your work based on urgency and importance.

- **Set Boundaries**: Establish clear times for communication—such as designated hours for meetings and email check-ins—and periods reserved strictly for deep work.

- **Leverage Technology**: Utilize software and apps that streamline communication and reduce time spent on unnecessary exchanges. This includes automatic scheduling tools and communication platforms that consolidate messages and files in one location.

- **Mindful Multitasking**: Understand that not all multitasking is efficient. Focus on one primary task while batching less intensive communication tasks, like quick email replies or instant messages, for specific, limited times during the day.

Practical Implementation

Implementing these strategies requires adopting specific habits and tools.

1. **Begin with a Plan**:

    ○ Start each day with a clear agenda.

    ○ List your tasks and assign them into categories based on priority and deadlines.

    ○ Allocate specific time slots for responding to emails and attending meetings.

2. **Communication Time Blocks**:

    ○ Block out times on your calendar for communication-related tasks.

    ○ Communicate these blocks to your colleagues to set expectations.

3. **Productivity Apps**:

    ○ Employ tools like Trello, Asana, or Monday.com to manage tasks.

    ○ Use Calendly or Doodle for scheduling without back-and-forth emails.

4. **Interruption Management**:

    ○ Use status indicators on communication platforms to signal availability.

    ○ Turn off notifications during deep work periods.

Implementing these strategies is not a one-off task; it's an ongoing process that demands discipline and flexibility to adjust as demands change.

Consistency and Evaluation

Sticking to a system is the linchpin of time management success. Be consistent in your methods, but also regularly evaluate your processes.

- Weekly reviews help assess what's working and what's not.

- Adjust your plan and tools as needed to improve efficiency.

- Maintain an open dialogue with your team about your time management strategies, ensuring they complement group objectives and respecting others' time as much as your own.

In conclusion, balancing communication with productivity is about setting priorities, establishing boundaries, adopting the right tools, and being adaptable. When you successfully manage your time, you not only boost your productivity but also enhance the quality of your communication, leading to a more harmonious and efficient work environment.

DECISION MAKING: COMMUNICATING CHOICES AND CHANGES

The Key Ideas

Decision making isn't just a solitary act of choosing; it's also about effectively communicating those choices and the subsequent changes they lead to. Clarity in communication ensures that your decisions are understood, respected, and executed properly.

• **Purpose Over Popularity**: Choose actions that align with your goals, not just ones that appease others.

• **Transparency**: Share the 'why' behind decisions to foster trust and reduce resistance.

• **Inclusivity**: Consider and acknowledge the impact on all stakeholders.

Practical Implementation

The way you communicate decisions can have a significant impact on how they're received. Here are steps to clearly and effectively convey decisions:

1. **Prepare What to Say**: Craft your message with care, ensuring it's straightforward and devoid of ambiguity.

2. **Choose the Right Channel**: Select a medium—email, meeting, video—that best suits the message's complexity and the audience's needs.

3. **Timing Matters**: Communicate your decision promptly, allowing time for implementation and adjustment.

4. **Concisely Why**: Include rationale to give context and help others understand the benefits or necessities of the decision.

5. **Anticipate Reactions**: Be ready to respond to feedback and provide additional clarification if necessary.

6. **Call to Action**: Clearly outline the next steps and expectations post-decision.

In the digital age, it's also important to address the etiquette of online communication:

• **Be Mindful of Tone**: Digital communication lacks the non-verbal cues of in-person exchanges, so choose your words carefully.

• **Respect Privacy**: When communicating sensitive decisions, consider secure and private channels.

Consistency and Evaluation

Maintaining a steady approach to both decision making and the way you communicate decisions is crucial for credibility and trust.

• **Follow Through**: Demonstrate the same values and criteria in each decision-making scenario.

• **Seek Feedback**: Regularly ask how your decision-making process and communication can improve.

• **Measure Impact**: Assess the outcomes of your decisions and how your communication impacted those outcomes.

Adjust your methods as needed to ensure that your communication remains clear, considerate, and effective. Remember, in the world of workplace success, it's not just what decisions you make—but also how you communicate them—that shapes your professional narrative.

BODY LANGUAGE: THE SILENT COMMUNICATOR

The Key Ideas

Unspoken Signals: Body language comprises the various signals our bodies emit, ranging from facial expressions to posture. It's a silent form of communication that often conveys more than spoken words.

Subconscious Messages: Many body language cues are given and interpreted subconsciously. Understanding these cues allows you to read between the lines in social and professional interactions.

Cultural Variance: Body language is not universal. Be aware that gestures, eye contact, and personal space have different meanings across cultures.

Synchronization: When your verbal and non-verbal cues align, your message is more powerful. Misalignment can lead to mistrust or confusion.

Practical Implementation

1. **Observe First:**

   ○ Spend time studying people, focusing on non-verbal cues.

○ Note how body language often aligns with the emotional tone of a conversation.

2. **Self-Assessment:**

○ Videotape yourself in a conversation to become aware of your body language.

○ Identify any habits that might be sending the wrong message.

3. **Practice Positivity:**

○ Engage in body language that exudes confidence, like standing tall and making eye contact.

○ Smile genuinely to foster trust and warmth.

4. **Adopt Active Listening:**

○ Show that you are listening by nodding and tilting your head.

○ Eliminate distractions, such as checking your phone during conversations.

5. **Control Nervous Habits:**

○ Be aware of nervous twitches or movements that can undermine your message.

○ Learn to keep them in check through mindfulness or stress reduction techniques.

Consistency and Evaluation

Regular Check-ins: Consistently assess how your body language aligns with your communication goals. Are you projecting confidence or causing doubt?

Seek Feedback: Ask trusted friends or mentors to provide you with honest feedback about your body language cues and their impact.

Adapt and Evolve: Be willing to adjust your body language for different situations. What works in a casual setting might not suit a formal presentation.

Evaluate Outcomes: After important interactions, reflect on what went well and what didn't. Were there moments when your body language may have conveyed a message you did not intend? Learn from these reflections.

EFFECTIVE USE OF VISUALS IN PRESENTATIONS

The Key Ideas

Visuals are your allies in storytelling—they punch up your narrative, reinforce your message, and make your content memorable. But like any tool, they need to be used skillfully.

• **Purpose-Driven Imagery**: Select visuals that underscore your central message. Every chart, graph, or image should serve a clear purpose.

• **Simplicity**: Keep it straightforward. Complex visuals can overwhelm and confuse your audience.

• **Quality Matters**: High-resolution images and crisp graphics project professionalism and credibility.

• **Relevance**: Your visuals must tie in directly with your presentation's content. Irrelevant visuals distract rather than enhance understanding.

Practical Implementation

• **Data Visualization**: Use charts and graphs to make numerical data relatable. Consider bar graphs for comparisons, pie charts for proportions, and line charts to demonstrate changes over time.

- **Infographics**: Great for condensing information and statistics into an engaging, comprehensive format. Use them to simplify complex ideas.

- **Use of Color**: Employ color strategically. Different colors can evoke specific emotional responses and highlight key points.

- **Text in Visuals**: Minimize. When you do use text, make it large enough to read and don't crowd visuals with words.

- **Animations and Transitions**: Use sparingly. Keep animations purposeful and transitions smooth to maintain professional polish.

Consistency and Evaluation

- **Design Consistency**: Stick to a consistent style—font, color scheme, layout—to maintain coherence throughout your presentation.

- **Evaluate Your Visuals**: Test their impact. Ensure they convey the intended message and enhance the viewer's understanding.

- **Feedback Loop**: After your presentation, solicit feedback. Ask specific questions about the effectiveness of your visuals to refine future presentations.

Visuals should complement your presentation, cementing your message in the viewers' minds without overshadowing the spoken word. Employ them thoughtfully, sparingly, and with intent to turn a good presentation into a great one.

COMMUNICATION AUDITS: SELF-ASSESSMENT FOR IMPROVEMENT

The Key Ideas

Conducting a communication audit is akin to a health check-up for your professional interactions. It's a reflective process aimed at scrutinizing the efficiency, effectiveness, and satisfaction within your communication practices. By committing to self-assessment, you acknowledge that even the most competent communicators can enhance their skills.

- **Identify Your Communication Habits:** Understand your current practices. Are your messages clear and concise? Do you listen actively? Recognize patterns and triggers that either aid or obstruct effective communication.

- **Set Clear Objectives:** Know what you want to achieve. Do you aim for better team collaboration? Or perhaps you're working on becoming more persuasive. Tailor your audit to meet these goals.

- **Assess Your Tools and Channels:** Evaluate the platforms you use for communication. Are emails, meetings, or instant messages serving their purpose, or are they cluttering the communication landscape?

- **Seek Feedback:** Incorporate perspectives from colleagues. An outside view can reveal blind spots in your communication style.

To start, keep a log for a week, and note down:

- Instances when your communication was misunderstood.

- Moments you felt unheard.

- Times when the outcome of an interaction didn't meet your expectations.

This log serves as a tangible reference for patterns that may emerge.

Practical Implementation

Armed with key ideas, putting them into practice requires a methodical approach.

1. **Break Down Your Communication**: Isolate different aspects of your communication—verbal, non-verbal, written, and digital. Evaluate each area separately.

2. **Design a Checklist**: Create a list of qualities that reflect effective communication in your field. Are your interactions empathetic, respectful, and clear?

3. **Self-Rating**: After dividing your communication into categories, rate yourself. Be honest and critical without being overly harsh.

4. **Create an Action Plan**: Based on your identified areas of weakness, decide on concrete steps to improve. This could include training, mentorship, or practice scenarios.

5. **Practice**: Implement these changes in a controlled environment before taking them into your professional sphere.

For non-verbal communication, consider:

- Eye contact during conversations.

- Gestures that either complement or detract from your words.

- Posture and body language that convey confidence.

Consistency and Evaluation

Improvement is a continuum, not a destination. It requires regular check-ins and adjustments:

- **Set a Review Schedule:** Determine regular intervals to reassess your communication. Monthly or quarterly audits can keep your skills sharp.

- **Use Quantifiable Metrics**: Whenever possible, measure improvements with data. Track the number of successful projects, reduced misunderstandings, or positive feedback received.

- **Adjust as Necessary**: Be flexible in your approach. If a strategy isn't working, pivot and try new methods.

Remember, every interaction is an opportunity to practice and refine your skills. With consistency, your communication will not only improve, but it will become more effortless and natural.

In summary, implement these strategies to turn your audit into a powerful tool for communication mastery:

- Maintain concise and meaningful exchanges.

- Stay responsive to feedback.

- Be adaptable in your strategies.

- Celebrate small victories; each step forward is progress.

Self-assessment is a powerful skill in itself. Harness this, and watch as your professional communication transforms, leading to increased influence, stronger relationships, and heightened success in the workplace.

HANDLING DIFFICULT CONVERSATIONS WITH CONFIDENCE

The Key Ideas

Difficult conversations are an inevitable part of professional life. Whether you're addressing performance issues, resolving conflicts, or providing constructive feedback, the goal is to handle these discussions with tact, clarity, and empathy.

- **Prepare Thoroughly**: Before initiating the conversation, define your objectives, anticipate responses, and consider potential solutions.

- **Active Listening**: Show you're receptive to the other person's perspective. Nod, maintain eye contact, and paraphrase to demonstrate understanding.

- **Emotion Management**: Keep your emotions in check. Practice staying calm and composed, irrespective of how heated the conversation may get.

- **Clear Communication**: Use simple, straightforward language. Avoid jargon or ambiguity which might lead to misunderstandings.

- **Empathy**: Acknowledge the emotional aspect of the conversation. Validate their feelings without necessarily agreeing with their stance.

- **Solution Orientation**: Aim for a constructive outcome. Focus on resolving issues rather than assigning blame.

Practical Implementation

1. **Prepare Your Approach**:
   - Define the issue in clear, specific terms.
   - Anticipate the other person's perspective.
   - Plan how to start the conversation.

2. **Establish a Safe Environment**:
   - Choose a private, neutral setting.
   - Ensure there will be no interruptions.

3. **Structure the Conversation**:
   - Begin with a positive, truthful statement.
   - Describe the issue without assigning blame.
   - Use "I" statements to express your perspective.
   - Invite them to share their thoughts.

4. **Manage the Flow**:
   - Steer the conversation back on track if it strays.
   - Keep interjecting reaffirmations of mutual goals.

5. **Conclude with Action Steps**:
   - Agree on tangible next steps.

○ Schedule a follow-up to assess progress.

Consistency and Evaluation

Maintaining a consistently confident approach to difficult conversations ensures that, over time, you'll be more effective in handling them.

• **Reflect on Outcomes**: After each conversation, take time to reflect on what went well and what could be improved.

• **Seek Feedback**: Ask a trusted colleague for their perspective on how you handled the conversation.

• **Practice Regularly**: Use role-play scenarios to build your skills.

• **Track Progress**: Keep a journal for milestones and lessons learned, to recognize patterns and improvement areas.

Remember, confidence in difficult conversations comes from preparation, skillful execution, and reflective practice. Each conversation is an opportunity to advance your communication mastery.

CURIOSITY AND QUESTIONS: TOOLS FOR ENGAGEMENT AND UNDERSTANDING

The Key Ideas

Curiosity isn't just a personal trait; it's a potent instrument. By harnessing curiosity, you can foster deeper engagement, enhance understanding, and develop more meaningful connections in the workplace. Questions are the catalysts for curiosity—prompting us to delve beyond the surface and explore possibilities.

- **Asking the Right Questions**: Learn to craft questions that spark dialogue and open lines of communication. Ditch the simple "yes" or "no" in favor of open-ended inquiries that require thoughtful responses.

- **Active Listening**: Display genuine interest by actively listening to the responses. This encourages further conversation and conveys respect for your colleague's viewpoint.

- **Encouraging Others**: Motivate coworkers to ask their own questions. This promotes a culture of inquiry and collaboration, pivotal for professional relationships.

- **Leveraging Curiosity for Problem-Solving**: Utilize curiosity to understand problems deeply and thus find more innovative solutions.

- **Building Connections**: Express curiosity about your colleagues. This isn't prying; rather, it involves showing an interest in their perspectives and experiences, which strengthens professional bonds.

Practical Implementation

Implementing a curiosity-driven approach requires a tactical blend of psychology and skill. Consider these steps:

1. **Begin with Open-Ended Questions**: Avoid those which can be answered with a simple "yes" or "no". Instead, ask how, why, and what questions to invite elaboration.

2. **Echo and Paraphrase**: Reflect back what someone says. This shows you're listening and prompts clarification.

3. **Express Curiosity without Judgment**: Approach each question with an open mind and refrain from premature conclusions.

4. **Follow-Up Questions**: These demonstrate you're engaged and interested in the detail, urging the conversation forward.

5. **Use Pause to Your Advantage**: Silences give others the chance to think and offer more nuanced answers, leading to richer conversations.

Consistency and Evaluation

To truly benefit from curiosity and questioning, embed them into your daily interactions. This isn't about using these tools sporadically; it's about fostering an ongoing culture of inquiry.

- **Set Personal Goals**: Aim for a certain number of meaningful questions in each meeting or conversation.

- **Solicit Feedback**: Ask colleagues if they feel heard and understood, adjusting your approach as necessary.

- **Reflect and Journal**: At the end of the day, review your conversations. Did your questions deepen understanding? How can you improve?

- **Consistent Practice**: Challenge yourself to remain curious, even when it feels easier to accept things at face value.

Regularly evaluate the impact. Are conversations more productive? Are relationships at work improving? Keep what works, tweak what doesn't, and maintain the pursuit of a curious and questioning mindset for continuous growth.

ESTABLISHING CREDIBILITY AND AUTHORITY IN YOUR SPEECH

The Key Ideas

Understand Your Topic Inside and Out

- Become an expert by doing thorough research.

- Update and refresh your knowledge regularly.

- Use statistics and facts to support your points.

Exude Confidence

- Practice your speech to master the content.

- Utilize confident body language.

- Speak clearly and at a measured pace.

Build Rapport

- Connect with your audience by understanding their interests and perspectives.

- Share personal stories or anecdotes when relevant.

Show Passion and Enthusiasm

- Demonstrate genuine interest in the subject.

- Let your tone reflect your enthusiasm.

Refer to Credible Sources

- Quote well-respected figures in the field.

- Cite current and relevant studies.

Project Professionalism

- Dress appropriately for the context.

- Use professional language and avoid slang.

Practical Implementation

1. Research Extensively

   ○ Dedicate time to understand every facet of your subject.

   ○ Keep notes of important points, studies, and expert opinions.

2. Rehearse Often

   ○ Conduct dry runs of your speech in varying conditions.

   ○ Record and critique your presentation.

3. Interaction Forward

   ○ Prepare questions to involve the audience.

   ○ Encourage open dialogue.

4. Continuous Improvement

   ○ Seek feedback from trusted peers.

   ○ Adjust your content and delivery based on constructive criticism.

5. Utilize Visual Aids

   ○ Employ graphs, charts, or slides to highlight key points.

   ○ Ensure aids are clear, professional, and accessible.

6. Manage Q&A Professionally

   ○ Anticipate possible questions and prepare answers.

   ○ Handle unexpected questions with poise.

Consistency and Evaluation

Daily Practice Regularly engage in speaking exercises to maintain a high level of performance.

Feedback Loop

• Implement a method to collect audience feedback after each speech.

• Use this information to refine and adapt your approach.

Self-Reflection

• After each speech, evaluate your performance.

• Identify areas for improvement and work on them before your next appearance.

Long-Term Growth

• Set goals for your speaking skills and work towards them systematically.

• Attend workshops or trainings to enhance your abilities.

Peer Observation

• Observe colleagues' speeches and take note of effective techniques.

• Apply observed successful strategies to your own presentations.

Accountability

• Commit to a plan for continuous improvement.

• Revisit your goals and progress regularly to ensure you stay on track.

SOCIAL MEDIA SAVVY: PROFESSIONAL COMMUNICATION IN THE DIGITAL AGE

The Key Ideas

Understanding the Platform

- Recognize each social media platform's unique etiquette.

- Identify your target audience and fine-tune your message accordingly.

Crafting Your Message

- Ensure messages are clear, concise, and tailored to the digital environment.

- Use appropriate language and tone that reflect your professional brand.

Building Relationships

- Engage with followers by responding to comments and messages.

- Share and comment on relevant content to foster community and industry connections.

Privacy and Discretion

- Be mindful of the public nature of social media.

- Avoid sharing sensitive or controversial information.

Practical Implementation

Profile Optimization

- Use a clear, professional profile picture and a concise bio.

- Regularly update your profile to reflect your current role and achievements.

Content Strategy

- Plan your social media content calendar.

- Develop a mix of original content and curated industry-related information.

Engagement Practices

- Set aside specific times for social media activity to stay consistent without compromising productivity.

- Monitor mentions and engage in conversations where your expertise can add value.

Measurement and Analysis

- Track engagement metrics to evaluate the effectiveness of your communication.

- Adjust strategies based on data-driven insights for continuous improvement.

Consistency and Evaluation

Content Consistency

- Maintain a regular posting schedule.

- Align all posts with your professional brand and message.

Brand Voice

- Craft a recognizable and consistent voice across platforms.

Social Media Audits

- Periodically review your social media presence and content for relevance and impact.

- Continuously refine your approach based on feedback and industry trends.

Network Expansion

- Seek opportunities to grow your professional network strategically.

- Use social media analytics to identify potential collaboration and expansion areas.

COMMUNICATION IN LEADERSHIP: INSPIRING AND GUIDING YOUR TEAM

BREAKING DOWN SILOS: INTERDEPARTMENTAL COMMUNICATION STRATEGIES

The Key Ideas

Interdepartmental communication is a critical component of a thriving workplace. It fosters collaboration, innovation, and a cohesive company culture. The cornerstone of breaking down silos lies in understanding that effective communication is not just sharing information but also ensuring it is received and understood.

Transparency is paramount. When each department understands the others' challenges and objectives, mutual respect is cultivated.

Accessibility is another important factor. Creating channels where staff can easily reach out to colleagues in other departments removes barriers.

Lastly, **initiative** from leadership and staff at all levels is necessary to promote and sustain interdepartmental communication. It requires continuous effort and active participation.

Practical Implementation

1. **Establish Clear Channels of Communication:**

   ○ Create interdepartmental meetings to share updates.

   ○ Implement a clear and accessible internal communication platform, like an intranet or a message board.

2. **Design Cross-functional Teams:**

   ○ Assign projects that require collaboration among different departments.

   ○ Encourage employees to contribute to teams outside their standard roles.

3. **Promote Social Interactions:**

   ○ Organize casual meet-ups or team-building activities.

   ○ Facilitate cross-department mentorship programs.

4. **Provide Training and Tools:**

   ○ Offer workshops on effective communication skills.

   ○ Supply resources that make collaboration seamless, such as shared digital workspaces.

5. **Encourage a Speak-up Culture:**

   ○ Allow employees to voice concerns and ideas without fear of retribution.

   ○ Create suggestion boxes or anonymous feedback mechanisms.

6. **Recognize and Reward Collaboration:**

   ○ Highlight successful cross-departmental initiatives.

○ Offer incentives for teams that work well together.

Consistency and Evaluation

Consistent application of these strategies is vital. Create a rhythm in interdepartmental communications – frequent enough to stay connected but not so often that they become a formality devoid of substance. Regularly evaluate the effectiveness of communication strategies through surveys and feedback mechanisms. Adjust approaches based on evaluation outcomes to ensure practical, evolving communication channels.

Remember: Success lies not in a one-time fix but in building a robust system of ongoing, dynamic interaction across all levels of the organization.

CONTINUING PROFESSIONAL DEVELOPMENT: STAYING SHARP IN COMMUNICATION SKILLS

The Key Ideas

Effective communication is a cornerstone of professional success. To maintain and enhance this vital skill set, you must engage in continuous learning and practice. Here's what you need to focus on:

- **Active Listening**: Treat listening as an active process. Hone the ability to fully concentrate, understand, respond, and then remember what is being said.

- **Non-Verbal Communication**: Regularly reflect on your body language, facial expressions, and tone. They can speak as loud as words.

- **Clarity and Conciseness**: Aim for brevity and clarity in your messaging. Time is valuable; respect it by getting to the point swiftly.

- **Empathy**: Understand and share the feelings of others. Communication is not just about exchanging information but also about connecting on a human level.

• **Feedback**: Provide and seek feedback. This two-way street ensures you stay aligned with how your communication is perceived and can improve it.

• **Adaptability**: Tailor your communication style to your audience. Recognize and adjust to cultural, contextual, and individual differences.

Practical Implementation

1. **Set Specific Goals**: Define what you want to achieve in your communication skills. Whether it's improving your presentation skills or becoming better at conflict resolution, setting clear objectives provides direction.

2. **Learning Resources**: Use books, podcasts, webinars, and workshops to build knowledge. Choose resources with actionable insights and practice exercises.

3. **Practice**: Implement what you learn in real-life scenarios. Role-play, simulations, and real-world interactions are crucial.

4. **Mentorship and Networking**: Connect with communication experts. Learning from their experience and receiving personalized advice can be invaluable.

5. **Reflective Journaling**: Keep a journal to reflect on your daily communication encounters. Identify what went well and what you could have done better.

6. **Online Courses and Certifications**: Enroll in courses that offer structured learning paths and credentialing. They can provide depth in specific areas like negotiation or public speaking.

Consistency and Evaluation

- **Regular Review**: Routinely revisit your communication goals and strategies. Are you making progress? What needs adjustment?

- **Measure Progress**: Create a set of metrics to gauge improvement. It can be as simple as getting more positive feedback or reducing misunderstandings in conversations.

- **Accountability Partners**: Pair up with a colleague or a coach who can hold you accountable. Regular check-ins with them can keep you on track.

- **Adapt and Evolve**: As you receive new information and your environment changes, be prepared to adapt your communication strategies. Stay nimble and open to evolving your skills.

In sum, refining your communication abilities is a lifelong pursuit. By integrating constant learning and deliberate practice into your professional life, you ensure that your communication skills remain sharp and effective, helping you to excel in your career.

WORK-LIFE BALANCE: COMMUNICATING BOUNDARIES FOR PERSONAL AND PROFESSIONAL WELL-BEING

The Key Ideas

• **Acknowledging the Need for Boundaries**: Understand that boundaries are not selfish. They are essential for maintaining mental health and sustaining high performance at work.

• **Articulation of Boundaries**: Clearly defining what your availability is, whether in terms of time, energy, or tasks, is pivotal.

• **Negotiation Skills**: Effective boundary setting is often a process of negotiation. This means being able to compromise without sacrificing core personal needs.

Practical Implementation

1. **Self-Assessment**: Start by listing personal priorities and professional obligations. Determine where conflicts arise and where boundaries could be drawn.

2. **Direct Communication**: Verbally express your boundaries to those impacted. Use "I" statements to take ownership of your needs.

3. **Written Clarification**: For professional settings, an email or documented agreement solidifies the communicated boundaries and ensures clarity.

4. **Prioritize Obligations**: Identify non-negotiable aspects of your job and personal life. This helps in communicating what can't be compromised.

5. **Set Specific Limits**:

    ◦ Define work hours or check-in times.

    ◦ Specify modes of communication after hours, if necessary.

    ◦ Clarify the urgency levels of tasks.

6. **Role Modeling**: Demonstrate the respect for boundaries by upholding others' limits. This can create a reciprocal understanding.

7. **Prepare for Pushback**: Not everyone will understand or respect your boundaries initially. Prepare responses to common objections in advance.

Consistency and Evaluation

• **Regular Reviews**: Revisit your boundaries regularly to assess their effectiveness and to make adjustments as your work and life evolve.

• **Feedback Loops**: Encourage open dialogue with colleagues, friends, and family about these boundaries to facilitate mutual understanding and respect.

• **Self-Reflection**: Regularly check in with yourself. Are you more balanced? Less stressed? Note the impact of boundary setting on well-being.

Remember, success in communicating boundaries lies in clarity, consistency, and the willingness to uphold one's own limits even in the face of resistance. This is not an exhaustive list, but a starting point on a journey to rediscovering your personal and professional well-being through effective communication.

CONCLUSION

As we come to the close of "Communication Mastery: 42 Techniques for Workplace Success," it's essential to pause and reflect on the journey we've taken together. You've navigated through layers of communication strategies, delving into the art of listening, speaking with clarity, and building bridges across cultural divides. By now, you're brimming with knowledge and practical tips, and you're poised to employ these techniques in your daily professional dance.

Recap of Key Takeaways

Let's underscore some pivotal insights:

- **Active Listening**: It's not just about hearing, but understanding. Remember, it's a skill that requires practice and patience.

- **Empathy and Non-Verbal Cues**: These are the subtle, yet powerful, undercurrents in the sea of communication.

- **Feedback and Emotional Intelligence**: They can turn a workplace from a battleground into a fertile ground for growth.

- **Conflict Resolution and Persuasive Communication**: When wielded wisely, they can transform disagreements into opportunities.

Implementing What You've Learned

- **Start Small**: Take one technique and commit to using it consistently until it becomes second nature.

- **Practice Mindfully**: Every conversation is an opportunity to practice and refine your skills.

- **Reflect Regularly**: Take a moment at the end of each day to consider what went well and where you can improve.

Make It Personal

Consider personal stories, like Jane, who defused a heated meeting by employing active listening, or Carlos, who won his team's trust through clear and empathetic communication during a company crisis. These are not just tales; they're testaments to the power of communication.

Communication is an Ongoing Journey

Here's a fact: communication is not a destination; it's a continuous journey. Like any master craftsman, you must keep chiseling away, honing your skills, and embracing new methodologies.

Looking Ahead

As you forge ahead with the tools and insights you've gained, remember:

- **Stay Curious**: Always be on the lookout for new communication techniques and insights.

- **Adapt and Evolve**: What works today may not tomorrow. Be ready to pivot.

- **Seek Feedback**: Relish in constructive critiques—they're goldmines for growth.

Final Words

In the tapestry of the workplace, your communication threads can either tangle in knots or weave a fabric of success. With the 42 techniques in your arsenal, you are now better equipped to ensure it's the latter.

As you leave the pages of this book behind and step forward, let the principles you've absorbed be the compass that guides your professional relationships and development. Here's to your success in becoming an adept communicator who not only speaks and listens but truly connects with others in the workplace and beyond.

Keep the conversation going, and may you master the art of communication with the grace of a seasoned conductor, turning each encounter into a harmonious symphony of ideas.

www.ingramcontent.com/pod-product-compliance
Lightning Source LLC
Chambersburg PA
CBHW071205290526
45796CB00008B/154

* 9 7 9 8 8 7 5 6 8 1 5 1 6 *